THE TRUTH

Written By:

Rev. Daniel W. Leighly
New World Horizons Ministry

newworldhorizons.net/divinelight.html

This Book can be purchased, and is available at: LULU Publishing at:
www.lulu.com/sevenkeys

Thank You and God Bless

THE TRUTH

Metaphysical Philosophy

Written by
Rev. Daniel W. Leighly

Printed in The United States of America

ISBN: 978-1-4303-2027-2

Publisher: LULU Publishing

THE TRUTH

Metaphysical Philosophy

Rev. Daniel W. Leighly
New World Horizons Ministry

Chapters

Chapters

Dedication

I dedicate this book to all who seek the TRUTH. For those who have longed for, and dreamed of a better life, a better way, or a Path to follow. Here are your answers.

You have the Power Within Your Consciousness. The Power of your Thoughts and of your Feelings to Create whatever it is that you desire.

The Natural Laws of Attraction, Right Action, Gratitude and Love are working within you now and once you realize the Secret or the way to harness this Energy, The World can be yours.

THE TRUTH

Introduction

You who have heard the call of your Inner-Self, that inner voice that beckons you to search, that inner light that shines upon your path. Now you will know the Truth.

You will share the **Secret To Life**.
This Secret is pure, Spiritual knowledge, and is approachable by anyone, from anywhere, at any time.

This Secret is the Divine Power of the Universe. It is The Law Of Attraction.
It is The Law Of Gratitude, It is the Law Of Right Action, and The Law Of Love.

These Laws govern your destiny, your future. These Laws are set into motion by your thoughts, your emotions, and your desires.

You have the Power to Create your World.

This Is The Truth.

Energy is timeless and has always been here. It illuminates for all of humanity the greatest material perfection, and the primary purpose of life, to attract and create Abundance.

This Energy is your access to everything that you have ever dreamed of. It is your ticket to everything that you have ever wanted. It is the Secret to Life.

All that is left for you to do is unlock the doors to your destiny, and use this knowledge to create the life you desire. You hold the answer to your dreams.

Within this book is the knowledge that you have been searching for, the answers that you have been longing for.
You will find within these pages the doorway to your Future.

It doesn't matter who you are or where you come from. It doesn't matter whether you are rich, poor, homeless, hungry, employed, unemployed, disabled, healthy, happy or sad.

We all use the same Energy.
We all have access to the same Power.
We all have Dreams and Desires, and we can all Create the World in which we live.

We can all start changing our futures **Now!**
You can start with nothing, and have everything.
Now, ask yourself this question.

Are you living life to the fullest?

If your answer is NO, or I'm Not Sure, or Not Really. Then ask yourself this.

Why Not!

Chapter One
The Essence Within

Our existence is based on the fact that we are all made up of energy.

Each human being possesses this energy, and it manifests in all creation through Divine Laws, Physical Laws, and Natural Laws that must be studied, respected, understood, and practiced for the greater good of Humanity.

In order to understand how it works, you have to visualize Intention. If you visualize this energy within you, then you have the power to direct your thoughts, and your intentions to create your destiny.

Visualization brings our thoughts into a closer realization of our reality.
You have the ability to create your life, and watch it manifest around you.

The World is evolving around this energy, and this energy can create all of the things that you think of.

Ask and you shall receive.

All people seek happiness, wealth, abundance, joy, freedom, good health, and love. The ability to have all of these things in your life is yours for the asking.

You only need to Believe!

The only way to fully experience this manifestation is by maintaining harmony within oneself, with other people, and with the Universe.

Everyone alive is using this energy, and if you learn to use it in the Correct Way, you will be able to manifest whatever it is that you want.

You must realize that it is you that has this power. It is you that can change your reality. All of your desires will be fulfilled, and your greatest fears will be dissolved if you change the way you think.

This is The Law Of Attraction.

The Core essence of The Law Of Attraction is the use of your thoughts in the Correct Way. It is not possible to achieve the goals you want or the desires you want unless you believe you have the Power to do so.

You cannot do all the things you were meant to do unless you have an Abundance of things. You need to have an abundance of Money. You need to have an abundance of Ideas, and you need to have an abundance of Faith, in order to secure your future.

You cannot have things to use unless you have an Abundance of Money to use.

You need to be Rich in order to have the life that you deserve. You need to know that an abundance of money is yours already. You just need to believe it.

You can do this with The Law Of Attraction. You have the right to a Full Life, full of everything that you could ever need to fulfill your dreams, and the goals that you are yet to accomplish. It is the power of your own thoughts, that will create your own future.

Chapter Two
Desire

You need to spend some time reflecting on what you want out of life.
In order to have what you want in life, you have to be ready to receive it.

In order to have a fulfilled life you need to have an abundance of everything.

If you desire something and you visualize it in your mind, and then you think about it with the belief that it is yours, The Universe will begin to manifest it for you.

All that is needed is your continual thought and intention to make it happen.

You have to believe that it is yours.
You have to be ready to receive it, and you must be thankful.

Gratitude is one of the biggest reasons that you can receive what you want.

The Law Of Attraction is always working. It never sleeps, it never stops, and it is always Creating.

Many people pray for better things in their lives, better circumstances, health, happiness, and wealth.

The problem is they don't really picture themselves having all this. They only see the outward appearances of their current circumstances.

In order for the Energy to work, you have to be able to visualize the results. You have to believe in Power. There can be no room for Doubt.

If you believe, so shall you receive. Positive feelings, and positive thoughts, bring about positive change.

This is the Truth.

The thoughts and words that run through our minds, that we speak with our mouths are very important.
What we believe and how we express it go hand-in-hand with how we receive the gifts that are available to us.

Everyday, if we can quiet our noisy minds of all the clutter in our material world, we can open up ourselves to our inner Spiritual realm. Then we can start to create a sense of what it means to be at one with ourselves, to find inner peace, and to be one with the Universe.

Give thanks to the Divine and know that The Energy Within will produce Perfect Results in your life.

See it within your own mind. Think of the way you want it to be, not the way you don't want it to be. Never give any energy to negative thoughts. Always think positive and maintain an attitude of gratitude.

The riches of the world are within your reach.

Chapter Three
Gratitude

Here are seven daily steps that you can use to show gratitude for all that you have.

1. In the morning, as you rise give thanks for the new day and look for things to inspire you throughout your journey. Then, take seven deep breaths as you focus on the vitality that is awakening in you, as you begin your day.

2. Make your life's mission Living with purpose and Respect the Laws of Nature. Be faithful to the promises and commitments that you make.
Consider it to be a precious gift to be alive.

3. Always consider life the most precious gift of all. Nature is the most beautiful sanctuary and expression of Divine Perfection on earth.

Respect life in all its forms, and look upon animals as sensitive, feeling and conscious beings and not as just living things.

4. Behave in such a way that all those who have contact with you regard you as an example of Light and the right way to live. May your first actions always be to think well, speak well, and act well.

5. Be generous towards all those who are in need or who are less fortunate than you. Every day do at least one good deed for someone.

Whatever your good deed, be thankful that you are able to contribute to the well being of others.

6. Regard all humanity as your family. Beyond race, culture, status, and belief, all human beings are brothers and sisters living within the same Universe.

Respect all religious and philosophical beliefs, as long as they are not directed against humanity.

7. As your day ends before going to sleep, reflect on the events of your journey. Search your Mind remembering what you have thought, said, and done throughout this day.

Then meditate on the lessons of your journey. When this is done, send positive thoughts and good feelings to all of humanity and entrust that the Universe will answer your call.

Gratitude is the use of the Power of Thought in a way that will put you in Harmony with the Energy of the Universe. The same way that there is a Law Of Attraction, there is a Law Of Gratitude.

You must learn to use this Law in order for The Law Of Attraction to work.

The Law Of Gratitude works this way. When you give thanks or praise for the things you already have, you make way for more to come to you because you are thankful. The Law Of Gratitude is a Natural Law and will always respond in a Like Nature. Remember Reaction and Action are always equal. The response you receive will be the same as you send out.

What this means is the Universe will give you more of the good things you deserve because you are thankful for all the good things you already have.

As you give thanks for what you have, you are saying that you are Happy and Pleased with what you have attained thus far. You appreciate the better things in life, and want and deserve more. The Energy of the Universe will comply with this, bringing more of the better things into existence.

You want the best in life; the best that life has to offer. Think these thoughts in your mind, and feel the best feelings that you can feel. See yourself with the best; the best of everything and that is what The Law Of Attraction and The Law Of Gratitude will produce.

Be Grateful for everything good that comes into your life, and more will come into your life as well. Be thankful every time you get a chance throughout your day. Expect the best; expect good things, and you will receive the best and more good things.

Showing Gratitude will bring more things into your life to be Grateful for.

Chapter Four
The Law Of Attraction

Metaphysics is a philosophical term, the literal meaning of which is the subject with which it deals is metaphysica, which means (behind the physics).

Metaphysics is a science that holds great knowledge. Like The Bible, which tells of many things both physical and Spiritual, the study of Metaphysics also reveals these same truths.

The Law Of Attraction is pure Metaphysics. Through Metaphysical study we find that the Spirit or Soul, and the physical body are one yet separate.

Your Thoughts Create Feelings, and Feelings Create Energy and Energy Creates Substance.

This Energy is all you need to create what you desire. Remember This:

Thoughts Create Things.

You can trust that what you think of now, health and abundance, loving relationships, joy, happiness, and success are yours for the asking.

The process of positive thinking is one and the same with the process of realizing the awareness and determining your direction.

The Law Of Attraction is not new. It has been around since the beginning of time, and will be around long after we are gone from this earthly plane.

Imagine, what will happen when you teach yourself how to focus the power of your Inner Energy, Your Mind. What will happen when you encourage yourself to imagine yourself in Abundance?

What will happen when you learn to meditate, and you see your reality created?

How you see yourself, and the world in which you live, is how the Universe will respond to you.

That Is The Law Of Attraction.

There is an Energy from which all things are made and it fills the entire Universe.
All Thought in this Energy produces the things that are imagined by the thought.

You can visualize things with your thoughts and by impressing your thoughts upon this Energy; you can cause these thoughts to be Created.
Your thoughts and your Feelings
Create your Life and your Future.

Thought is the only Power that can produce these riches from this Universe.
No thought can be expressed without causing the Creation to Manifest.
Your Thoughts and Feelings Create Your Life.
You need to shift Your Awareness.
You need to Ask, Believe and Receive.
This is The Law Of Attraction.

There is Only Joy
There is Only Love
There is Only Good
There is Only Peace
There is Only Health
There is Only Freedom
There is Only Abundance
There is Only Fulfillment

You have the Power To Create Your Life.
Thoughts can Create Change.
Regardless of the Appearances,
Hold on to the Thought of Truth.

Thoughts Create Feelings.
Feelings Create Emotions.
Emotions, Feelings and Thought
are Energy.
Energy Creates Life.
This is The Law Of Attraction.
Thoughts Become Reality.
Know this is the Truth.

Feel Good, Have Good Thoughts.

I want to be Rich
I want to be Happy
I want to be Healthy
I want to be Fulfilled
I want to be Successful

Focus on What You Want,
and you will Attract it to Your Life.
Thoughts Cause Feelings.

I Am Rich
I Am Happy
I Am Healthy
I Am Fulfilled

I Am Successful
I Love Life
Life Loves Me

This is The Law Of Attraction.
Thoughts Become Things.

You Can Change Your Life.

Always be Positive about Everything you Need.

Write down your True Dreams and Goals and Focus on them.

Never Stop Believing.

Be Grateful for All You Have.

Give Thanks at Every Opportunity.

Think Only Good Thoughts.

Know that You Feel Good.

Refuse To Think Negative.

Your Thoughts Create Your Desires.
Your Desires will become Reality.

Chapter Five
Creation

If you will use these lessons on a consistent basis, you will see great changes in your life. You will find that your life will be fulfilling, and your desires will come true. Your world will begin to change around you, and right before your eyes the miracle of creation will be delivered.

Follow the sequence below:

1. Be Positive
2. Be Thankful
3. Feel Happy
4. Be Joyful
5. Act Successful
6. Feel Rich
7. Love Life
8. Be Fulfilled
9. Give Thanks
10. Feel Powerful
11. Be Determined
12. Feel Prosperous

Send out positive energy to the Universe in everything you do. The Law Of Attraction says that whatever you think, whatever you send out with thoughts and actions, will return to you.

Think Positive Thoughts:

I Am Happy
I Am Rich
I Am Successful
I Am Fulfilled
I Am Healthy
I Have Abundance
I Feel Great
I Love Life
I Have Financial Freedom
I Have More Than Enough Money
Everything Is Good
I Have Everything I Want
I Love My life
I Feel Young
I Feel Alive
I Am Full Of Energy
I Am Beautiful
I Can Reach Any Goal
I Can Realize My Dreams
The World Is At My Service

Visualization is the process and the ability to create clear, powerful, mental images. It is one of the most important steps in creating the reality of your desires.

All great accomplishment begins with a thought, an idea. That thought is then reinforced through the action of concentrated feelings, and begins to develop into inner self-power or vibration.

If these thoughts are strong enough, clear enough, and consistently reinforced, eventually they will become reality.

Visualization takes time to develop, but once mastered through practice can often lead to a greater understanding of The Law Of Attraction, and is the Key to Materialization.

Visualization is the ability to create a clear, well-focused image, and hold it in the mind.

A clear mental image, in order to be effective must be concentrated on regularly with intense feelings.

One must practice the ability to create crystal clear, sharp images with color, texture, sound, and full depth of dimension.

You want to make these images as real as possible. When you do this the level of vibration transforms into energy.

This energy is transferred into the Universe and is set in motion to manifest the results back to you.

The key to manifestation is The Power Of Thought and the concentrated Feelings that empower the Universe to Act.

This Is The Law Of Attraction. The thoughts you have and the feelings that you put behind those thoughts are what determine that which is created in your future.

You are the creator of your future. It is all up to you what you have, and what you don't. You are in control of your thoughts.

Think About That!

Chapter Six
Sanctuary

Each of us has a Sanctuary where we can go to find our own true peace. Below is a simple Metaphysical exercise to show you how to enter this inner realm of tranquility.

The Inner Sanctuary

Find a quiet place where you will not be disturbed for at least half an hour. You may sit on the floor, or if you prefer, you may use a comfortable chair or lie down.

Close you eyes and take seven deep breaths. Allow yourself to relax as completely as possible. Take some time to release, any points of tension throughout your body. After a few moments try to clear your mind of all thoughts.

There will be an awareness that seems to be calling to you. Allow yourself to follow this call. Remain relaxed.

After a while you will come to a place that feels right to you. Allow yourself to remain in this place for a time. You will recognize it as a place of pure inner peace.

In time allow yourself to begin to explore this place in which you find yourself. Eventually, you will come to realize that this is your place of complete rest where you may safely and completely relax your mind, body and spirit.

This will be your place to rest, a place to renew energy where you may tap into the infinite life force of the Universe.

This Sanctuary will be unique to you alone. It's design and the way you visualize it will emerge from your inner nature. For some it may be a quiet garden, for others a temple for worship or a private retreat in the mountains. You will come to know this special place, your inner Sanctuary, where you will find complete peace and harmony. Remain relaxed.

Continue to explore your Sanctuary. You may find that there are hidden places, some containing treasures, some containing visions, all a part of your inner reality,

with which you must come to know, as your journey continues. Remain relaxed.

In the weeks, months, and years ahead you will return to your Sanctuary many, many times. You may build it in any image you wish. You may create it in whatever manner you desire, using your powers of concentration and visualization. You may also find that you will meet your Spiritual guide, (Your Inner-Self) if you do, don't be alarmed, listen to your inner voice.
This is your connection to the Universal Consciousness. Your Connection with The Essence Within.

This is your Inner Sanctuary. It is yours, and yours alone. It is a place of refuge, of clarity, of rest and rejuvenation, a place of great knowledge and Spiritual Wisdom.
This is your Temple, your place of Inner Light, a place to find your answers. A place to do great work.

You can retreat to your Sanctuary at any time. You will be able to find you're way quickly and easily to this special private place.

Only you have the Key.
As you continue on your path, whatever it may be, allow this Sanctuary to remain with you as an inner resource. Over the years, with further study, many powerful uses for this profound tool will show themselves to you. Remain relaxed, and Enjoy!

Don't Forget To Breathe.

Chapter Seven
Affirmations

Below are some positive statements and affirmations that you can use to create positive energy within your life.
Repeat these often as to quiet your mind and enter the Silence of your Inner Sanctuary.

1. I listen and hear only the Inner Voice, which speaks clearly and definitely to me.

2. I seek only the Positive forces in my life, so that I may attract to myself Happiness, Health, Success and Wealth, and all good things.

3. The Energy within me is producing perfect results in every phase of my life.
I now recognize, accept, and follow the divine plan of my life, as it is revealed to me.

4. The Energy within me is Creating Miracles in my Body, Mind, and Spirit. Positive Energy goes before me and prepares the way.

5. Everyday, In Every Way, I Am Better.

6. All that I will ever need is already mine.

7. More Money Is Coming To Me Now!

8. I Am Truly Grateful For All That I Have.

9. I Am a Very Successful Person.

10. I Can Have Anything I Want.

11. Everything That I Need Will Be Provided.

12. I Live In Abundance.

Divine Love

I stand alone on a deserted beach, the ocean waves around my feet, as the cool clear water rushes in, with the sound of the water meeting the shore.

The most beautiful sunset I have ever seen lights up the sky, as a magnificent array of colors mingle with the clouds.

The wind is soft on my skin as I feel the touch of its caress. Just as the sun kisses the horizon time stands still, and out on the water I see the reflection of God. His hands outstretched to show me all that He has created.

I am one with His Spirit; I am one with the Earth, and I am one with His True Love.
At this moment I realize that I am not only with God, but that God is with me, and all of this is His doing.

Rev. Daniel W. Leighly

Chapter Eight
Fulfillment

Even though the years have brought me to a place in life where I can now truly understand where I am and why I am here,

I sometimes still look out at the horizon and wonder if everything that has taken place in my life was my doing or the work of a greater force.

Questions will be answered if you look hard enough for the answers. Lessons will be learned no matter which path you choose. All will be revealed as life goes forward, and maybe if we really take the time to try and discover whom we are, will we find a meaning and a reason for life, as we know it.

The Truth is a book about Life's Journey. Every breath we take is a gift, every second we live is an event, and every day that passes is our story unfolding. Dreams can come true, and Love is the cure for all of the misfortunes we face.

As you turn the pages of this book I hope you find this to be true. I hope you find that Love is all we need to create a perfect world. I hope you discover the Secrets that wait, the answers to your questions, but most of all, I hope you find Yourself.

The dreams that you have can be fulfilled if you take the time to understand one vital truth. The Law Of Attraction, The Energy that surrounds us all is there for you to use.

Every thought you have has energy, and every time you send out those thoughts the Energy Responds.

Good or Bad does not make a difference to the Energy. It will create and manifest whatever you send out.

What you see in your life right now is what you created with the thoughts that you had.

What you will see in the future will be created from the thoughts that you have right now.

If you start right now and change your thoughts, you will change your future.

Chapter Nine
Imagine

Everyday brings a new meaning and a new way of seeing the world we live in. Time passes by without a thought to who we are or where we are going.

As our life moves forward we leave behind traces of our existence and ourselves. Long after we leave this earth our message can still be heard, but only if we take the time to make sure that we are not forgotten.

Imagine for a moment that you have just arrived on a distant planet. What would be your first impressions? What would be your first thoughts? What would you want to do first?

All that is before you is a brand new world. Everything that you now take for granted is in reality not what you really know. Imagine that for the first time in your life you will experience the world as it really is, as it was meant to be.

You are not seeing what is right before your eyes.

It may seem to you that this statement is far fetched, but in a short time from now you will start to see the reality of this message. You have the Power to change the World, and your Destiny. **Imagine That**.

Have you ever really taken the time to see what is really out there? Most people don't realize all that they miss. As you go throughout your daily routine you tend to ignore what is going on except for a small part that you include yourself in.

As you live, breathe, walk, talk, and experience everyday, life is all around you. You only see a very small part of what in reality is there. Picture this.

Your mind is constantly reacting to your environment. If you could play back what your eyes actually see, like a movie, and then sit and watch everything that has taken place around you. Only then would you realize that you haven't really seen but a small part of what your mind captured.

There is only a fraction of what your mind absorbs that you are really conscious of. The details that are taken in and actually stored in your brain are far more than your senses can comprehend.

There are avenues that you can take to create an awareness of your surroundings and a realistic approach to living in a more conscious state.

The details and aspects of your everyday existence are about to change. You are about to begin a journey that few have taken. You are about to discover a way to see yourself in a different light.

You are about to find out how to change your direction, your destiny, and most of all, your awareness of yourself.

Imagine what the possibilities are, and then reach out for them. They are within your reach.

As you will discover, there are tools that you can use to increase your awareness and understanding of your existence. These tools are within your mind.
These tools are held within the center of your being and can be called upon at anytime.

All that you need to know is that you have the power to use these tools at will, and once you do,

Things will start to reveal themselves to you.

As you continue your journey through the pages of this book, you will start to see that everything has a purpose, and everything has a reason for being.

As you master these techniques, you will be entering into a new realm of existence. You will be heading in a new direction. You will be finding a new reality, and for the first time in your life you will start to see what you have been missing.

Life has many mysteries and many secrets that for the most part are never known by the average individual. Now you have a choice to make.

You can go on living the same way that you have been, or you can take a Leap of Faith and discover for yourself what life is all about. You can discover for yourself a new beginning, a fresh look, and a clean start to a life full of hope. This is a New Horizon.

The Choice Is Yours.

Chapter Ten
Expect The Best

Always expect the best. You deserve the best of everything, and the Energy will bring it to you. One of the most Powerful Forces is Expectation. Always expect what you want in life. All the good things that you need to be happy, and all the rewards that are rightfully yours will be created.

By giving thanks to the Universe, you will send out a positive signal that you are thankful, and deserve all the best things in your life.

Use The Law Of Attraction everyday, and use it often throughout the day. If you get in the habit of thinking good thoughts, and having positive feelings, the Universe will respond to your vibration.

Think thoughts of wealth, abundance; feel as though you are already wealthy. See the money in your hands, in your bank account. Know that it is there. Feel the joy of buying anything you desire, and the money will appear, it will manifest.

You will attract into your life what you think about most. It could be Money, Health, Freedom to Travel, or Happiness.

Anything that you want can be realized if you just use the Energy Within You.

The Law Of Attraction Creates what you think about most.

If you think about what you don't have, then that is what the energy you are sending out is going to return to you, exactly what you have. What you see in appearance is what you have created with your past thoughts.

Until you change those thoughts your life will remain the same, whatever that is.

Picture yourself with a new car, a new house, and a huge bank account. Everyday see it in your mind, and think it in your thoughts. Feel as though it is already yours.

Believe it is yours and feel the joy of actually living the dream. Send out the positive energy that you deserve what you want, and the Universe will respond to the vision that you have.

If you tell yourself that you can't afford something or you think it would be to hard to own, then guess what, it will be.

Tell yourself that you can afford anything you want. It doesn't matter if you can or not. Just tell yourself that you can, and say it with conviction. I can afford that!

I can have that, I can do that, I can be that, I can feel that, I can see that, I want that, and it is mine.

Lack and limitation are only in your life if you think that they are. You can change your destiny. You can create the future that you deserve, the life that you want, if you believe that you can and you act like you can.

There is nothing stopping you from achieving your dreams. There is nothing stopping you from reaching your goals. Lack and limitation are part of your past.

The future is what you make it.

Many of you will have already grasped the illusions to see that life is a system of timeless growth. To strengthen that thought, let me say this as clearly as possible. Consciousness is the basis of what you are. It is your presence in this current life. Beyond your career, you're relationships, your accomplishments, and your desires. You are what you are conscious of.

The purpose of your being here is so that you can come to the full realization, and Clear Awareness, of the Oneness of yourself. The full impact of this statement may be hard to fully understand, but it must be clear that the purpose of this Life, and the path that you are on, has all been created by your thoughts.

Life is a continual process of growing Self-Awareness and the Essence of Life is that you create your own existence. If you will focus on your feelings, your creativity, and on the things you love, you can begin to take control, and to create the nature and quality of the events in your life.

You have the choice, you can select from all the potential paths of success in your future.

Chapter Eleven
Feelings

Your emotions are Powerful, and your feelings are essential to using the Energy Within to create what thoughts you send out. Every positive or negative thought that you have is charged with emotional energy.

How you feel about something, and how you perceive your existence is the key to change. If you continually think that you are not getting what you want, then that is what you will continue to get, and that is not what you want.

You have to change the way you think. You have to visualize and picture exactly what you want, and how you want it to be.

Then with all your emotions and all your feelings you have to see yourself receiving it. Feel good about it. Enjoy the moment. Know that it is already yours, and give Thanks.

Gratitude is the Secret to getting more of what you deserve.

When you are truly thankful for all that you already have, you open up the doorway to receive more.

Giving thanks needs to be a priority in your life. You need to establish a habit of giving thanks for everything in your life. Every time you give thanks, you send out a positive energy flow that The Law Of Attraction will always return to you.

The more thankful that you are, the more times you send out that positive feeling, the more the Universe will create for you.

You have to feel with your heart. You have to see the good things in your life and know without a doubt that you deserve more.

You can create your life any way you want. You can have anything that you want. You can achieve any results, as long as you send out the positive feeling that it is yours by default.

Use The Energy Within to Create Your Life.

The Universe is a Feeling Universe. Your thoughts and emotions Vibrate with Energy. This energy is the fuel that is needed to start the wheels in motion.

As you think and create feelings in your life, you send out the signals to the Universe to respond. Once you figure out this one little detail, everything will fall into place.

Take a piece of paper and find a quiet place. Sit down and really think about what it is you want in your life. What are your dreams made of? What do you want more than anything else? Write It Down.

Now close your eyes and picture it in your mind. Create a picture that is alive with every detail. Picture it in vibrant color, sound and movement. See yourself there, actually living in the picture. Feel the Joy of having this picture of your life come true.

Now, Believe that it is yours, and give thanks for the blessing. Say it out loud that this picture is your reality. Have No Doubt that the Universe is Creating it for you.

For The Law Of Attraction to work for you, you have to live the dream. You have to feel as though it is already happened. You must see yourself with the picture you have just created, and you must trust that it is already yours.

Don't waste your time trying to figure out how it is going to happen, just know that it is. All you have to do is Believe and Receive.

The Law Of Attraction never fails to deliver. The energy and thoughts that you send out are being created automatically. Whatever it is that you think will come back to you in reality. If you always think good, good is what you receive. If you think good health then good health is what you will have. If you think that you are rich, then rich is what you will be.

Don't ever think that you Lack anything. Always think you have Abundance of Everything, and always be Grateful for all that you have.

If you are grateful for what you have, the Universe will give you more.

Never limit yourself. Not to anything.
Do not let the appearances of your current conditions dictate your future.

You are a Powerful Human being bursting with Energy. You can radiate that energy, and direct your thoughts to create for yourself the perfect life.

Everything in your life right now is the manifestation of past thoughts. Whatever it was that you were thinking in the past is gone and has returned to you. Start today and change the way you think.

Only think right this time. Think about what you want. Think about the possibilities, and make them your center.
Channel your energy into your thoughts, and create the feelings of Abundance.

See yourself with everything you ever dreamed of. Reach out and believe that it is yours for the taking. The Universe will respond and will answer your request.

Thoughts Become Things so think about the things you want, and never stop thinking about your inner most feelings and desires.
The Universe will Respond.

Chapter Twelve
Abundance

Some people think that there isn't enough for everyone to have all they want in life. That there isn't enough money, or there isn't enough food, or there aren't enough jobs for everyone. The Universe has more than enough to share with everyone. There will always be more than enough to go around because the Universe has Abundance.

The Universe is Abundance. All of the energy that ever existed is still here. It never goes away, it never runs out, it always continues, and it is always creating more. More of everything.

If you spend your time thinking that there isn't enough, then you will never have enough. It doesn't matter what it is you are thinking about, there just won't be enough for you, because that is what you think, and that is what the Universe gives you.

If you think you are poor, than you are. You say I'm Poor, I'm Poor, I'm Poor, and the Universe answers Yes You Are Poor.

Now turn that around and say the opposite, I Am Rich, I Am Rich, I Am Rich, and the Universe will again answer, but this time it will say Yes You Are, You Are Rich!

The Law Of Attraction simply gives you what you ask for. You create what you want with your Thoughts and Feelings.

If you get in the habit of thinking of what you want and not what you don't want, you will be on your way to changing your entire life.

You create your life with the thoughts that you have. So change the way you think, and you will change your life.

The secret is not just thinking what you want. The secret is thinking as though you already have it. Don't think I want a New Car; think I have a New Car.

Don't think I want more Money, Think I have more Money. Lots Of Money!
The Universe doesn't care how big you think, it just responds to the thought.
So if you want Money, see yourself with Plenty. **Think I Am Rich**

Chapter Thirteen
The Truth

Truth can set you free. How little we realize what this statement can mean until we find out what the Truth really is. The Truth is a reality that few people alive today use.

We all are part of a Universe filled with Energy. What most people don't know is that they can use this energy at will. This energy is what creates all manifestations in the entire world. Your thoughts are what make this energy work for you.

Knowing this truth won't help you unless you apply it to your life. The actions that you take, the way that you choose to use this truth, are what determine the outcome of your reality.

The Laws that are explained in this book are all a part of the Truth that must be used in order to make what you want in your life a reality.

On the next few pages I will list for you a guideline on how to use these Laws and this Truth to create your reality.

There have been countless books written on the subject. Ages ago men discovered this Truth and throughout the centuries it has been used by a select few to accomplish their dreams.

Some of the greatest people who ever walked the planet used these Laws and knew the Truth of the Power they held.

That Power is within you. That Energy that is the life of all creation is within you. You can harness this Power, this Energy, and by doing so can create a life of Abundance in everything you touch.

History repeats itself time after time but the Truth is always the same. Whatever you Desire can be yours if you follow these Laws.

The Law Of Attraction, The Law Of Gratitude, The Law Of Right Action and The Law Of Love.

The Truth is that The Law Of Love is what binds all the other Laws together.

These are The Laws Of The Universe, These are what **The Truth** is made of.

Here is where you are, standing at the threshold of your existence. You are at the doorway to your future, your reality and what is next on the path of life.

It is time to ask yourself some questions. As for the answers you are given will come only from the true Source of the Truth within you.

You must know that what I am saying to you right now at this very second, is that you are what you say you are. You are what you see yourself as. Your dreams, and your thoughts, and your feelings are what you make through your use of this truth.

You create your Life.

What you do from this moment, how you act, what you think, what you feel and how you live will cause the Universe to respond to your wishes. You have to see this Truth. You have to see this reality. Unless you wake up and grasp hold of the Golden Ring that is before you, you will miss your turn.

Open The Doorway To Your Future.

Below are some questions that you can use to open this doorway. Write them down and study them. Take the time necessary to answer each one as completely as you can. Then after you are satisfied with the answers, seal them in an envelope and put them away for safe keeping.

Someday you may want to review them, or share them with someone. Either way put them in a safe place, and step through the doorway to your future.

1. Of all that you have experienced in your lifetime, what is the most enjoyable feeling that you can remember?

2. If you could only make one wish come true, what would it be?

3. Who Do You Love?

4. What do you truly desire out of life?

5. How can you improve the world.?

6. What makes you happy?

7. What makes you sad?

8. Do you desire more?

9. How much money is enough?

10. Can you make your dreams come true?

11. Where did everything you have right now in your life come from?

12. Are you doing what you want?

13. Is your life fulfilled?

14. Are you healthy?

15. Are you successful?

16. Do you enjoy work?

17. Do you have friends?

18. Do you believe you have the power within your-self to change?

19. Do you want to change?

20. What is stopping you?

I do not know what you wrote down as your answers. I do know that those answers will determine what you do or don't do with the rest of your life.

I am now going to give you some answers of my own. These answers are given for one reason only. So that you can see what these questions are meant to do for you.

As you read these answers, compare them to your own and see if we don't have something in common.

1. Of all that you have experienced in your lifetime, what is the most enjoyable feeling that you can remember? I think that the most enjoyable feelings that I can remember are the days when my children were born.

2. If you could only make one wish come true, what would it be? I would wish for an end to world suffering, and that everyone alive today could benefit from and share a Universal Love.

3. Who Do You Love? I love my wife, my family, my children, I love myself, and I love God.

4. What do you truly desire out of life?
I want to be fulfilled in everything I do.
I want to make a difference.

5. How can you improve the world.?
I could improve the world by sharing my ideas and by writing more books.

6. What makes you happy?
Music, Laughter, Good Food, Loving Feelings, Learning and Living.

7. What makes you sad? War, Hatred, Violence, Anger, Sickness and Poverty.

8. Do you desire more? Yes, I desire more of everything life has to offer.

9. How much money is enough? When I can fulfill all of my dreams and desires then I will have enough money.

10. Can you make your dreams come true? Yes, I am already making my dreams come true.

11. Where did everything you have right now in your life come from? Everything that I have right now in my life came from my past thoughts.

12. Are you doing what you want? I am in a continual process of moving forward to doing what I want.

13. Is your life fulfilled? So far yes.

14. Are you healthy? Yes, I am healthy.

15. Are you successful? I am Successful.

16. Do you enjoy work? I love to work.

17. Do you have friends? I have many friends.

18. Do you believe you have the power within your-self to change? Yes, All that I need to change is within my own power.

19. Do you want to change? Yes, and I am changing.

20. What is stopping you? **Nothing!**

Nothing can stop you either!

That Is The Truth!

Chapter Fourteen
The Laws

The Universe is life in motion. Every single aspect made up of Energy. Everything you see, touch, taste, smell, and hear is energy in motion.

This Energy is the **Secret To Life**.
You have within yourself the Power to Create your Destiny.

The energy that you create within the power of your thoughts is sent out into the Universal Vibration of Manifestation.

The Universe is constantly creating form and substance from this energy.

Your Thoughts, Your Dreams and Your Desires are real, and can be created with the power of your mind.
Remember this:

The Power of The Universe is Within You.

The Law Of Attraction simple states that whatever you think of and desire the most you will attract. This means that if you think of money, and having money, and know that you deserve lots of money, you will have money. It won't appear overnight, or automatically appear in your bank account.

What will happen is that the Laws of the Universe will start to manifest that which you desire. It will start to make the changes in your life, and align the energies that you send out. You will start to attract the things that will bring you money.

You can't just sit back and wait. You have to act. What I mean by that is something, maybe something very small or unpredictable will happen, and unless you act in the right way to work with the Universe, nothing will happen.

Everything is a part of this Energy. Every time you want something, every time you think about something the Universe wants to give it to you.

You have to be ready to receive it.

Here is an example: I want to have more money, so I say to myself, I want more money. I start to think about having more money. I plan on getting more money and I know that the Universe is working to make it happen. The wheels are set in motion so that I can have and make more money.

The next thing I know is that my boss calls and says that they need me to work some overtime. Overtime? I have a choice. I can say yes and work the overtime or I can say no, I am to busy and I want my time off.

What has just happened here is that the Universe was working with me to have more money. Depending on my choice I can make more money or refuse to act towards that goal.

If I decide to take the time off instead, I get exactly what I want, more time off. Not more money. This is a simple example but it is always the same no matter what it is that you want. The Universe will respond to you.

I never know what is going to happen next in my life. Sure I have an idea of what to expect, but what I mean is that the wheels of the Universe are always in motion.

You have to be ready to act in order to receive that which you have asked for.

Lets say that I decide to work the overtime. I go to work and put in my time, and all the while knowing that I am making more money. Not just my regular salary but time and a half. Right before I am ready to leave for home I realize that I need something at the store. While entering the store I see an ad on the wall that says looking for someone who wants to make more money!

Is that ad for me? Should I call that number? Should I act? Is this just a coincidence or is this The Universe answering my call?

The Universe creates the things that you desire. That doesn't mean that the Universe will drop a bank-load in your living room. What the Universe will do is start in motion the wheels of manifestation. The Law Of Attraction will start to work in your favor.

People, Ideas and Things will start to come forth, and once they do, who knows what will happen.

The Law Of Attraction Works For You.

Chapter Fifteen
Right Action

What do we mean by Right Action. Right Action is anything that you do to move forward in your quest for what you want.

You have to act right, think right, feel right, and be right in everything you do. The Universe has no other choice but to respond back to you in a like manner.

All that is needed on your part is the Right Action. When you know what you want, and you truly desire it with all your heart, and you put out those positive feelings that you can achieve it. The Universe will start to create that which you are thinking of.

That is Right Action.

You have to be sure, and you have to be clear. Being clear is a very important part of Right Action. If you can visualize what it is that you are after, and clearly get it straight in your mind. It Is Yours.

Clearing is a process by which you rid your mind of any and all so-called doubts.

By focusing on with all of your intentions that which you truly wish to create, you set the right frame of mind to achieve your goal.

You must believe in yourself, and you must believe that you have the power within you to make it happen. When you think of something in your mind, and you focus on it intently, giving it feeling, you are acting in the right way.

Right Action is No Doubt, No Fear, and No Second Guessing. You know that what you want, and what you desire can and will be yours because it is designed that way.

Every second of every day the Universe is creating something from the energy that surrounds us all. There is more than enough energy just within yourself to create everything that you have ever dreamed of.

The time to act in Now! The time to change is Now! The time to see your dreams come true is Now! Start acting in the right way. Start doing what you feel is right. Start believing that you can and guess what, you will.

That Is Right Action.

Chapter Sixteen
Will Power

Do You Have Faith? This is a hard question to answer. Faith can be many things to many people. You could have faith in God. You could have faith in Yourself, and you could have faith in the Universe.

Maybe you are one of those people that says faith is up the Powers That Be.

What you need to do is to realize that YOU are the Powers That Be. You have the Power Of The Universe at your disposal. You can tap into the Energy of All Creation, and you can do it from within your own mind.

Will Power is just that, Power Of The Will. All of us have it. It is called Free Will. We have the will to do as we see fit. We have the freedom of choice. What you need to see is that this free will that you have, is a very powerful tool that can be used whenever you want.

Will Power can move Mountains. It can Change the World. It can **Create Your Destiny.**

Once you realize the power of the mind everything will change for you. Your world will change, and the way you think will change. Everything that you say and do, you will do with a purpose.

That purpose will be to create your future. Your Will Power is as strong as you can imagine. Nothing can get in your way once you start to use this power. The energy within your will can create an explosion of feelings and emotion, this combined with the truth, and your thoughts, will harness the energy that surrounds you, and manifest the reality.

The power of your mind is all you need to bring forth the powers of the Natural Universe, and use the Natural Laws that are here for you to change you life.

Believe in yourself, trust in the Power of your Mind, and let the Laws of the Universe manifest your desires.

It starts with you, and it ends with you. You have already what so far you have wished for. Change your wishes, and you will change your existence.
Change your thinking and you will create your future.

Use the Power of your will to change your destiny. Start today and use the energy within you to change your life. Everything that you think from this day forward let it be positive, let it be good, let it be joyous, and let it be abundant.

Use the Universal Laws of Creation to make your dreams come true. Use the Power of your Imagination to Fulfill your Desires.

Know that you are great, feel that you are wonderful, know that you are deserving, and clearly see yourself with abundance.

Think properly and use right action. Be determined that you can make it possible. Know in your heart with all your emotions that the Universe will provide. Then watch as the miracles occur in your life. Watch as the Universe unfolds with you.

Be Grateful for everyday, Be grateful for all you have, Give thanks and praise for all that is coming, and behold the manifestation of your creative mind.

Watch, as your thoughts become your reality.

That is the Secret to Life.

Chapter Seventeen
It All Comes Back To You

It all comes back to you. Every single speck of energy that you put forth will come back to you. Think of it as gravity, only gravity in reverse. If you drop something it will fall.

That is the Law Of Gravity. If you get beneath a glass of water and then tip it over, the water will fall, only it will fall on you.

What you want to do is align yourself with the Forces of The Universe. You want to set yourself up so that everything that you send out to the Universe comes back to you.

The Secret is only sending out the thoughts of what you want, of what you desire. When you send out these vibrations into the Universe, the Natural Laws will send them back. It never fails.

Just like the Law Of Gravity works, likewise the Law Of Attraction Works. It will always give back what it receives.

The Bible says to treat others as you wish to be treated. This is The Law Of Attraction.

There are many examples that could be given, the Law Of Karma, what goes around comes around. Opposites attract, reap what you sew. What you give so shall you receive. It is all the same; it is The Law Of Attraction.

Like attracts like. If you give out happy thoughts, the Universe will give you more to be happy about. It's that easy.

Some of what I am saying may sound simple to you, but believe me it is some of the hardest work that you will ever take on.

To retrain your mind and to establish a new way of thinking takes time and determination. Most people give up after a few weeks or a few months because it is just to hard for them accept that they are making any headway.

People today live in a world of immediate satisfaction from the Internet to the way we shop. No one wants to wait for anything.

An old saying that comes to mind is: "Patience is a Virtue", but the one I like best is "Good Things Come To Those Who Wait".

Chapter Eighteen
Your Own Conscious Power

One of the things that people seldom realize is that they have their own conscious power. We are trained from the day we are born that we have to work to survive. We live in a world of pain and suffering, and of poverty and chaos. Everyday there is more bad news, and it seems that the world is for the most part, caught up in the cycle of self-destruction.

Only those who dare to seek the truth of what the world really has to offer, ever stand a chance of having a life of significance.

We are schooled in a way that is self - defeating. We teach our children to study the past, yet we hide the facts of what the past can really teach us. There is no positive thinking in our schools, and there is no hope for the future of our children, unless we start to teach them they are part of the bigger picture.

We have to begin to teach our children that they are the World. They are the Universe.

Only then will we see a change in what the world has become. There are millions of people out there, all made up of the same energy that you are made of. All of those people are putting out signals. A lot of those signals for the most part are negative. Not because those people want to consciously put out negative vibrations, but because they are surrounded by them.

Every negative word, every negative thought, every negative feeling goes out and returns. Most of those people are not conscious of this fact. They allow it to continue because it is ingrained in them.

Watch the TV, read the paper, listen to the radio, and you will hear negativity. Unless you consciously block those signals out, your sub-conscious mind absorbs them.

What happens then is that your sub-conscious mind starts to save these images. These images are stored, and begin to manifest as energy that in turn, is sent out to the Universe.

The Universe in response sends it back.
It is a vicious cycle.

In order to reverse this negative energy we have to reverse our thought patterns, and start overriding our sub-conscious minds with our conscious minds.

Your Own Conscious Power is hundreds of times stronger than your sub-conscious power. Positive thoughts always cancel out negative thoughts.

It has also been proven that positive thoughts are much more powerful than negative thoughts, and can be used exactly for that purpose. To eliminate negativity in our Universe.

Know that you have the Conscious Power within you mind to do and think any way you want. Knowing this fact, why would you ever not use it to better your life, and the lives of those around you?

You are your Own Conscious Power.
You have the ability to change your future.
You have the knowledge to Create your Destiny. Now the only question is, Will you?

Chapter Nineteen
Your Inner Self

Did you know that the Power of the Universe is within you? If you believe in God, or you believe in an Ultimate Power, A Higher Intelligence or a Universal Force that guides your destiny, than you have to know that this Power which you believe in comes from within.

You are part of this Universal Energy. You are a part of the process of creation. What you think with your mind, and what you have in your heart, is what you send out to the Powers of All.

Creation is a process by which energy is transformed into a manifested substance. What you think of most, and what you desire the most, The Universal Law Of Attraction will create.

This is the only way that it can be. This is the way that it has always been. There is no other way that life can survive. You will always attract that which you think about most.

Knowing this to be the reality, do you want to change your present situation? Do you have all that you need? Are you willing to create a better future? Now is the time to begin.

You have to look at the facts laid out before you, and ask yourself what do you believe?

There is nothing that I can do further to help you along your journey. Every single living Soul must make the decision on their own. I cannot do it for you.

I can show you the way, I can give you advice, but only you can act upon that information. Only you can choose to do what you know is right for you.

The doorway to your future is waiting to be opened. Only you have the Key. This doorway is your connection to all that is in the Universe.

Humanity is evolving towards the realization of a Divine Plan, and you are destined to Create your place in this Plan.

Within yourself are the **Answers You Seek**.

Chapter Twenty
The Path

What is the path that you are on? Where will it lead? What does your future hold in store?

These are Universal questions that we all have at some time in our lives. The answers will always be different for every individual, and the results for the most part, will always be what we expect.

Once you see what this means to your future, you will want to change the way you live. What you expect is always what you get. If you choose a path of hardship, you will have a long and hard road to travel. If you choose a path of sorrow, then you will forever be unhappy. Your Path is what you choose.

If you never knew any different, and you never were told that there was a better way, you may not ever find it. The difference here is that you have been told, you have been shown, and there is no turning back.

From this day forward you will know that what you have is a direct result of how you think, how you act, and how you live.

You are on the threshold of your future. From this day forward you can decide to be whatever you choose to be.

You can be Poor, Hungry, Lonely, Sad, Tired, Depressed, Angry, Mad, you can be Sick, Live in Fear, Disappointed and Bitter, or you can change your entire outlook.

You can Be Rich, Fulfilled, Loved, Happy, Full of Energy, Excited, Joyful, Caring; you can be Healthy, Full of Hope, Reassured, Forgiving, Successful, Wealthy, and Satisfied.

Your Path is what you choose. Your Destiny is what you Create. Your Life is in your Hands. Your Future is what you make it.

The Power of the Universe is at your Command. You must choose which path to follow. You must decide what change is necessary. You can believe in whatever you want to, or you can choose not to believe at all.

I choose to believe in myself. I choose to believe that there is a Greater Power at work in my life.

I choose to know that I am the solution to my problems, and that the answers that I seek are within myself. I know that there is an Inner Light that shines for me, that the Power of the Universe is with me now.

I choose to believe in God, and for me there is a comfort in knowing that all my prayers will be answered. All of my dreams will be fulfilled, and all of my desires will be attained.

There is no doubt in my mind that I can achieve anything. The Universe is at my Command.

The answers are there for those willing to look. The Universe will provide everything you seek. The inspiration comes from knowing the Truth.

I know the Truth of the Universe, I know the Power that it holds, I know that God is within me, and I know that my life will be created exactly as I wish.

The Laws have been written and will always be. The only thing that will ever change is how you choose to change it.

Chapter Twenty-One
The Secret

Through the ages of time and from the depths of your mind, you are discovering what can happen when you apply the Secret in this book.

The Laws of the Universe are the Secret To Life. Many have used them, and many have seen, how the Power Within transformed their lives.

This Secret has been passed down since the beginning of time. Many have hidden this valuable knowledge, others have sold it for great sums of money. To all who learn the Secret, The Universe is at your service.

The Universe is You, and You are the Universe. Energy and Vibration, Substance and Form. We are all a part of this Universal Existence.

The Secret is that You have the Power within yourself to change your Destiny.

What you think, say, do, feel, and how you act, live, dream, and create with your mind, is what you will get in return.

You can study all the books that have been written throughout time, The Bible, The Torah, The Koran, Metaphysical Journals, Scientific Articles, Plato, Einstein, Kant, Edison, and others.

All will reveal the same truths, the same results, and the same Secret.

The power to change your future is within you. Only you can create your life.

It is as simple as that, believe in yourself and start living your dreams. The Universe is on your side. It is all up to you.

There is but One Power in all The Universe, and that Power is within yourself. All the Energy that has ever existed in time is at your fingertips.

You Control your thoughts, and you Control your actions. The Universe will respond to your Desires.

Chapter Twenty-Two
Your Destiny

Your life is what you will make of it, because you have the Free Will to choose. Every decision that you make, every day that you live, every way that you act, and everything that you feel, your mind is constantly working, sending out the signals for the Universe to react.

You are an important part of this Universe. You can make a difference in this world. Every living Soul has a responsibility to the future generations of this planet.

Thought is your communication with the Universe. It is your way to acknowledge the Energy within. You can use this Power, this energy for your greater good, but you can also use it as service for the greater needs of humanity.

Only God knows what will unfold within our future lives, but you can help to create it.

The Truth has been told. May All Your Dreams Come True.

Peace Be With You.

Conclusion

Where is your future heading?
If you really take the time to answer this question, you will find that your future is within you.

Within You, is the Power and Energy to change your Destiny.
Everything you see and touch, everything surrounding you, from the air you breathe, the food you eat, to the sun you feel on your skin, is made up of Energy.

Think of the Love you feel when you hold a hand. Think of the way you feel when you kiss a child. The deep inner emotions and feelings that drive our consciousness.

This is your Life; this is created by your thoughts, your energy.

Imagine what it would be like if you looked out on the vast ocean and didn't see any water. Now think about how you would feel if you never saw a star.

What would the world be like if there was no music? What if tomorrow all the trees were gone, every blade of grass, and every plant and flower dried up and blew away.

What would the world look like then? How would a future artist ever paint a landscape?

Where would we be if there were no animals? What would you eat if there were no fruits and vegetables? How many salads can you make with dirt?

We take for granted this world, this life, and this wonderful place where we live. God planned it all, every last grain of sand. Every plant and every animal, every fish and every seed, and He did it with His Mind, with His Thoughts, with His Intentions.

Be Grateful.

Start using the Energy. Start right now! Think of the future you want to have. Visualize and Picture it in your mind. Start feeling good about it, and know that it is yours.

Know that you deserve it. Know that the Universe will Create it for you in Abundance.

Peace Be With You.

About The Author

Rev. Daniel W. Leighly

As a devoted Metaphysician and Founder of The Divine Light Ministry and New World Horizons Ministry.

I have studied for more than 30 years in the areas of Religion, Metaphysics, and Eastern Philosophy.

I hold the Title of Doctor of Metaphysics along with Bachelor, Masters and Doctorate Degrees "Honors" in Metaphysical Sciences and Philosophy.

I am an active Minister, Spiritual Counselor, and a Metaphysical Practitioner, dedicated to fulfilling Life's Purpose through my continued studies of the Universe, and by Serving Humanity in The Light of God.

New World Horizons Ministry

New World Horizons Ministry is a
Community Outreach, Holistic Spiritual
Sanctuary, founded by:
The Rev. Daniel W. Leighly.

We seek the Truth of our Existence through the study of Spiritual and Metaphysical Teachings that Encourage and Enlighten all of Humanity.
We believe in The Natural Laws that exist within our Universe, and we seek Harmony between these Laws and Ourselves.

New World Horizons Ministry
newworldhorizons.net/divinelight.html

Peace Be With You

If you enjoyed this book, please recommend it to your family and friends; all of my Books can be purchased,
and are available through,

LULU Publishing at:
www.lulu.com/sevenkeys

Thank You and God Bless,
Rev. Daniel W. Leighly

Notes

Notes

Notes

Notes

Notes

Notes

www.ingramcontent.com/pod-product-compliance
Ingram Content Group UK Ltd.
Pitfield, Milton Keynes, MK11 3LW, UK
UKHW040558210726
13854UKWH00008B/1489